MY CARIBOU
MIGRATION JOURNEY

BY NANCY LOEWEN   ILLUSTRATED BY PAULA ZORITE

PICTURE WINDOW BOOKS
a capstone imprint

Published by Picture Window Books, an imprint of Capstone
1710 Roe Crest Drive, North Mankato, Minnesota 56003
capstonepub.com

Copyright © 2025 by Capstone. All rights reserved. No part of this publication may be reproduced in whole or in part, or stored in a retrieval system, or transmitted in any form or by any means, electronic, mechanical, photocopying, recording, or otherwise, without written permission of the publisher.

Library of Congress Cataloging-in-Publication Data is available on the Library of Congress website.

ISBN: 9780756585365 (hardcover)
ISBN: 9780756585525 (paperback)
ISBN: 9780756585532 (ebook PDF)

Summary: Follow a caribou of the Porcupine herd on its magnificent migration journey.

Designer: Dina Her

Any additional websites and resources referenced in this book are not maintained, authorized, or sponsored by Capstone. All product and company names are trademarks™ or registered® trademarks of their respective holders.

Printed and bound in China. 6096

I was only born yesterday, but I can already run faster than any human being.

See all my playmates? They were born this week too!

It's late spring, and we're by the coast of the Beaufort Sea in northern Alaska. These are our **calving grounds**.

Here's my mother. Aren't her **antlers** cool? She'll shed them soon. Then new ones will grow in. Caribou are the only deer whose females grow antlers.

I'm a female too. Female caribou are called cows. I weighed about 13 pounds (6 kilograms) at birth. When I grow up, I'll be about 3.6 to 4.6 feet (1 to 1.4 meters) tall at the shoulders. I'll weigh about 200 pounds (91 kg).

Male caribou are called bulls. They weigh about 400 pounds (181 kg).

I can **graze** when I'm just two days old. But I still drink my mother's milk for a month or two. During the spring and summer, we eat grass and all sorts of leaves. Mushrooms are tasty too!

Not all caribou **migrate**, but my **herd** does! Every day we graze and walk. We can travel up to 50 miles (80 kilometers) a day.

11

Now it's midsummer. I'm bigger and can run even faster! Sometimes, I run just to get away from the bugs. Mosquitoes on the **tundra** are the WORST.

We gather together and stay close. The bugs aren't quite so bad this way. And we're safer too. We have to watch out for **predators**, such as wolves, wolverines, grizzly bears, and golden eagles.

My herd is called the Porcupine herd. That's because our calving grounds are by the Porcupine River in Alaska. We are a type of caribou called barren-ground caribou. There are more than 200,000 caribou in my herd. Just look at all of us!

Migrating the way we do is good for the land. Our **hooves** are big and hollow. When we walk, we make dents in the ground. They let in air and water for plants.

Even our poop is good for plants! It's full of **nutrients** that enrich the soil.

You're welcome, plants!

I love summer in the tundra! But we can't stay long. Soon, the plants will stop growing. We head south looking for food.

Graze and walk, graze and walk, graze and . . . SWIM! Sometimes we cross rivers. Our hollow hooves make handy paddles.

Fall is mating season. The bulls fight for mates. I hear the clacking sound of their antlers.

After mating season is over, most bulls lose their antlers. New ones will grow in. Male antlers can get really big. Some have more than 40 points, or branches!

By late fall, we've reached the snowy mountains in northern Alaska. We go where the food is. We may walk on the **plains**. Sometimes we go into the forests.

We spend much of our lives in snow, but we don't mind. Our fur keeps us warm.

During winter, I dig for my dinner. My hooves work like snow shovels. This time of year, caribou eat a plant called **lichen**. We are the only **mammals** that can eat it.

Our noses are special too. When we breathe, they heat up the air. It's like we're breathing in summer air, even on the coldest winter day!

We slowly head east into the Yukon Territory of Canada. When winter is almost over, we walk faster. We head back to the place where I was born.

We're here! This year I'm at the edge of the calving area. In another year or two, I will be in the middle, getting ready to have a calf of my own.

We've covered a great distance this past year—more than 1,500 miles (2,414 km)! We walk more than any animal in the entire world. And next year we'll do it all again!

ABOUT THE AUTHOR

Nancy Loewen grew up on a farm in southwestern Minnesota, surrounded by library books and cats. She now lives in Saint Paul and has published more than 140 children's books. Her Writer's Toolbox series received a Distinguished Achievement Award from the Association of Educational Publishers. Nancy has two adult children and a cat who sometimes nips at her knees under the table as she writes. Learn more at: nancyloewen.net.

ABOUT THE ILLUSTRATOR

Paula Zorite is a digital artist based in Valencia, Spain. She studied fine arts at the Polytechnic University of Valencia, where she discovered her passion for illustration. Paula has worked with a variety of authors and companies, creating vivid illustrations. Her style is characterized by a rich and harmonious use of color and a strong sense of narrative.

GLOSSARY

antler (ANT-luhr)—one of two bony structures that grow on the heads of animals in the deer family

calving grounds (KAV-ing GROWNDS)—an area where female caribou go to give birth

graze (GRAYZ)—to eat grass and other plants

herd (HURD)—a large group of animals that live and move together

hoof (HOOF)—the hard covering on an animal's foot; more than one are called hooves

lichen (LYE-ken)—a flat, mosslike plant that grows on trees and rocks

mammal (MAM-uhl)—a warm-blooded animal that breathes air; mammals have hair or fur; female mammals feed milk to their young

migrate (MYE-grate)—to travel from one area to another on a regular basis

nutrient (NOO-tree-uhnt)—something usually found in food, that is needed by a living thing to stay healthy

plain (PLAYN)—a large, flat area of land with few trees

predator (PRED-uh-tur)—an animal that hunts other animals for food

tundra (TUHN-druh)—a cold area in the far north where trees do not grow; the soil under the ground in the tundra is permanently frozen

INDEX

Alaska, 6, 14, 22, 27
antlers, 7, 20, 21

Beaufort Sea, 6, 27
bugs, 12, 13
bulls, 9, 20, 21

calving grounds, 6, 14, 28
Canada, 26, 27
cows, 7, 8, 10

eating, 10, 11, 18, 19, 22, 24

fur, 22

grazing, 10, 11, 19

hooves, 16, 19, 24

lichen, 24

mating, 20, 21

noses, 25

poop, 17
Porcupine herd, 14, 27
Porcupine River, 14
predators, 13

size, 8, 9
swimming, 19

tundra, 12, 18

Yukon Territory, 26, 27